SOUTH SHIELDS, WALLSEND, NEWCASTLE and BENWELL
In the days of the Romans

by
FRANK GRAHAM

Illustrated by
RONALD EMBLETON

I.S.B.N. 0 85983 156 6

© 1980

Published by Frank Graham, 6 Queen's Terrace, Newcastle upon Tyne, NE2 2PL

Printed by Howe Brothers (Gateshead) Limited

SOUTH SHIELDS

South Shields (or ARBEIA in Roman times), although south of the Tyne was part of the Roman Wall defences. It was basically a seaport and supply depot with a large civilian settlement.

The fort was probably built about 129 A.D. in stone during the reign of Hadrian when the system of northern defences was being established as the Roman Wall. Pottery has suggested a Flavian origin but if so the fort must have been sited somewhere else on the hill top. When Severus came north in 208 A.D. the fort was turned into a supply base with a very small garrison. Fourteen granaries have already been found. When the Scottish campaigns were over the fort returned to its former use and some of the granaries were changed into barracks. An inscription shown below records the building of a new aqueduct in 222 A.D. by the Fifth Cohort of Gauls.

The "Aqueduct Stone"

The fort seems to have been abandoned late in the 3rd century and not used again until well into the 4th. The last coins found in the fort are two of the Emperor Arcadius who reigned from A.D. 395 to A.D. 408.

The original 2nd century garrison seems to have been a cavalry regiment the *ala Sabiniana*, 500 strong followed by the First Ala of Asturians (name mentioned on a tombstone). An inscription mentions the 5th Cohort of Gauls at the beginning of the 3rd century with, later in the 4th century, a unit of Tigris Lightermen (numerus Barcariorum Tigrisiensium) mentioned in the *Notitia* along with the name of the fort ARBEIA They were probably only here for a short time since South Shields went out of use by *c.* 400 A.D. These bargemen were probably used for ferrying troops and stores up the Tyne.

The fort in its final form measures 620 by 360 feet covering an area of just over five acres. Its defences are a stone wall backed by a turf rampart with a gateway in each of its sides. In front are two ditches.

A very large collection of Roman material has come from the site. There are two magnificent funereal monuments. The one to Regina, with its inscription in two languages (unique in Britain), is shown here.

The funereal monument to Regina

The first part of the inscription is in Latin and reads in translation—"To the divine shades. To Regina a freed women and (his) wife, Barates a Palmyrene (erected this monument. She was) by nation a Catuallaunian, (and lived) thirty years." It ends with a line in the Palmyrene language, translated—"Regina, freedwoman of Barates, alas!" Regina is shown with a distaff and spindle in one hand while the other raises a decorated chest supposed to hold her personal possessions. At the other side is a basket containing weaving materials. Barates was a mechant who supplied military standards and his own epitaph was found at Corbridge where he died aged 68 years.

It has been suggested that this tombstone was the work of a Palmyrene living at South Shields. Being a large seaport and an important civilian settlement Shields would have had a large polyglot population.

The domestic scene recorded on this funereal monument is shown on our coloured plate (Page 16).

Tombstones are the most common of all remains surviving from Roman times. There were special workshops of monumental masons where stocks were kept of various designs and at different prices. The relations would select the stone they liked and the name of the deceased and suitable words would be inscribed and then painted in red. Such a scene is shown by R. Embleton. (Page 13). The masons would also manufacture temple altars, some of which are shown in the drawing.

Roman funerals were elaborate affairs. The dramatic picture shown on page 20 illustrates a funereal procession of a wealthy inhabitant of *Arbeia*. The people depicted are, from left to right — family mourners and friends, slaves carrying the *lectus funebris* funeral manager (*Dissignator*), hired mourners (*Praeficae*), flute players (*tibicines*).

Roman ship passes Tynemouth on its way back to Rome

However Shields was not the centre of the funeral trade on the wall. It had a thriving commerce, some local manufacturers, and numerous shops. One of these trades was the manufacture of jet ornaments many of which have been found along the Wall (See Vindolanda). Our illustration shows a jet worker at his bench The methods of manufacture and the tools used were almost identical with those employed at Whitby in the last century (Page 17).

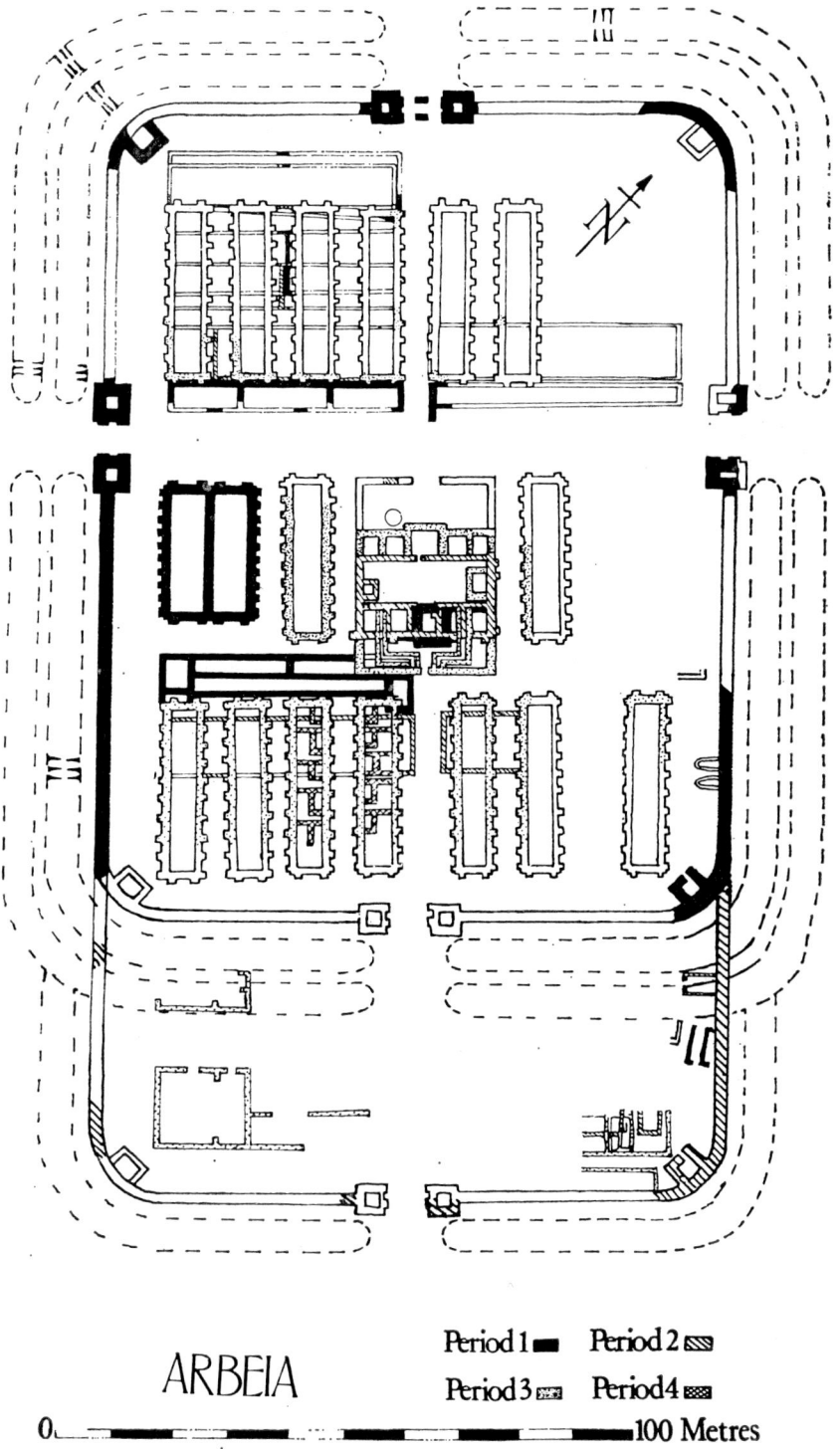

Plan of Arbeia. By kind permission of Tyne and Wear Museum Service

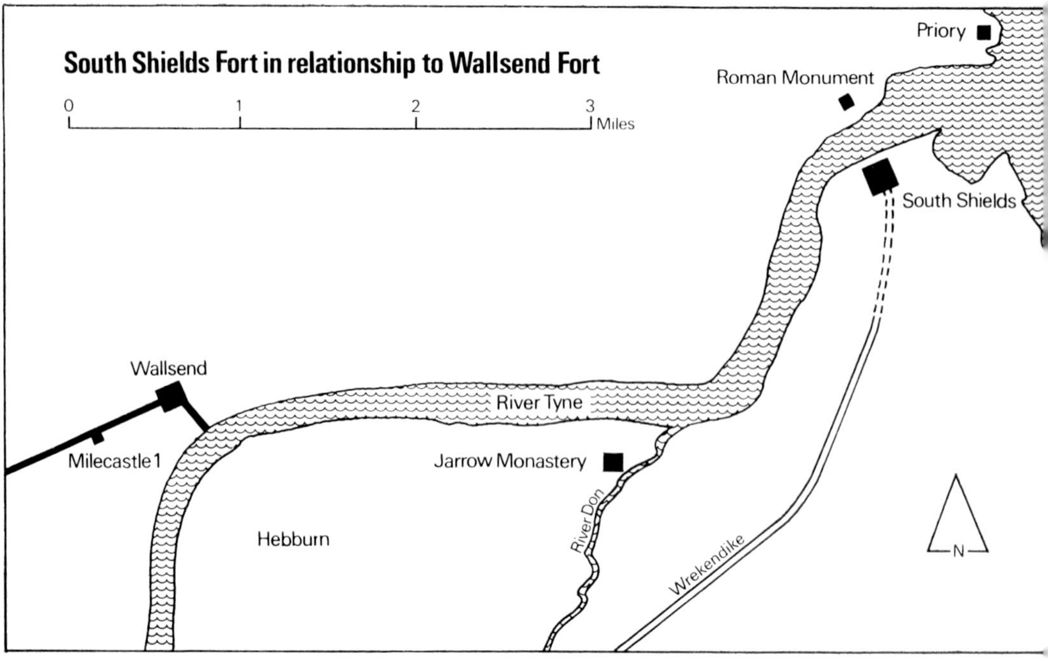

South Shields Fort in relationship to Wallsend Fort

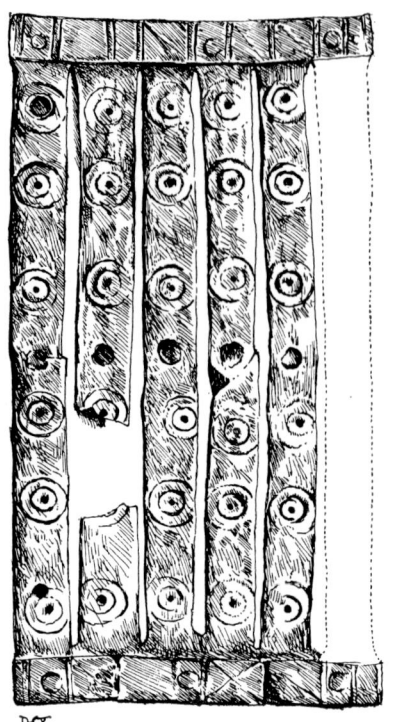

At South Shields an interesting domestic article has been found in a good state of preservation. It is a bone weaving frame, and consists of a perforated bone plate with silver mountings, rather small, being only $3\frac{1}{2}$ x $1\frac{1}{4}$ inches in size. It is a heddle frame used for weaving narrow bands of material such as belts, head bands and decorated cloth for embellishing women's clothes.

HADRIAN'S WAR MEMORIAL

The Roman Wall, with its camps, roads, towns and villages was the greatest single building achievement of the ancient world. The men who planned and executed this great mural barrier must have been proud of their work. The emperor Hadrian would almost certainly have erected some monument to record his achievement. His patron and predecessor Trajan had built a magnificent war memorial on the eastern front to commemorate his victories there and to mark the boundary of the Roman Empire. His enormous monument at Adamclisi in modern Rumania has now been completely restored in all its magnificence..

The eastern and western ends of the Wall were probably chosen by Hadrian for identical monuments. At a later date Severus may have recorded his rebuilding of the Wall with a memorial near the centre. Was the huge "mausoleum" outside Corbridge, near the main Roman road north, the work of Severus?

In 1866 when the nave of Jarrow church was being rebuilt two inscribed Roman stones, used by the original Saxon builders, were discovered. One of the stones was finally presented to Burlington House, London and the other to the Blackgate in Newcastle. In 1943 Ian A. Richmond and R. P. Wright published an article in *Archaeologia Aeliana* suggesting the two stones belonged to a monument erected by Hadrian after the Wall was built.

The original inscribed stone was probably six feet square and formed part of a large war memorial or *tropaeum*. Although less than quarter of the original inscription was left the two authors were able to suggest more than half of it. The Blackgate fragment (with the additions) in translation reads:-

> *The emperor Caeser Traianus Hadrianus Augustus son of all his divine ancestors, decided it was necessary on the advice of the gods to fix the boundaries of the Empire in the second consulship . . .*

OMNIVM · FIL
AIANVS HADR
ITA NECESSITAT
VATI DIVINO PR
S11

Roman lettering on the Blackgate fragment. (words in italics have been suggested).

The Burlington House fragment tells us:-
> *The barbarians were scattered and the province of Britain freed. A boundary was established between the two oceans a distance of 80 miles. The army of the province built the Wall under the command of Aulus Platorius Nepos imperial legate and propaetor.*

DIFFVSIS
PROVINC
BRITANNIA · AD
VIRVMQVE · O
EXERCITVS · PR
SVB CV R

Roman lettering on the Burlington House fragment.

If I. A. Richmond and R. P. Wright are correct where would this monument have been. Clearly not at Jarrow. It was too low lying and of no importance. Shields could have been the site but the fort itself stood on the highest land and such a war memorial would not have stood out. Tynemouth is clearly the place and the Collingwood Monument or the Priory probably stand on the spot. The *tropaeum* would have been clearly visible from the large base at South Shields and also to every ship that entered the Tyne.

When the Saxon church at Jarrow and the medieval priory at Tynemouth were built Hadrian's memorial would have been a good source for stone and was probably completely removed.

Ronald Embleton's reconstruction has been based on the monument at Adamclisi.

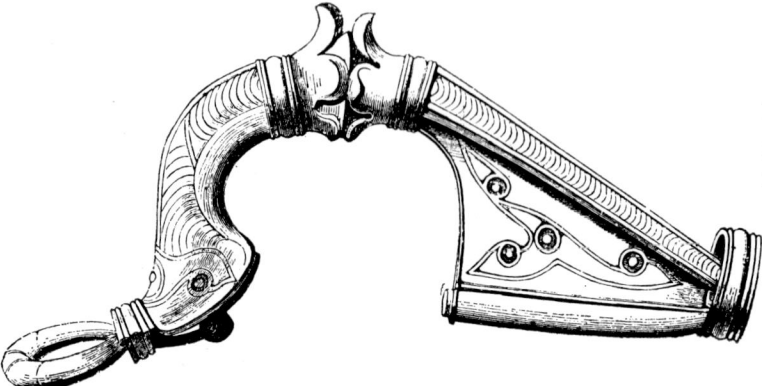

A siver gilt *fibula*, used to hold parts of a garment together. Celtic in style it almost certainly came from somewhere on the lower Tyne.
(Part of the so-called Backworth Hoard).

FIBULA FOUND AT BACKWORTH. (FULL SIZE.)

WALLSEND

Wallsend, as its name implies was at the east end of the Wall. The *Notitia Dignitatum* puts it first on the list, under *Item per lineam valli*, as *Tribunus Cohortis quartae Lingonum Segeduno*. The name is Celtic and signifies a *hill* of some kind. The fort occupies a good site, with a wide view in every direction, and being on an angle of the river dominates the stretches to the east and west. We do not know the original garrison but in the second century the Second Cohort of Nervians was stationed here. In the third and fourth centuries the part-mounted Fourth Cohort of the Lingones were here. Both garrisons were 500 strong.

From the south-east angle of the fort the Wall continued to the river and extended into the stream at least as far as low water level. In 1903 part of this Wall (6 feet 6 ins. wide) was discovered and re-erected in Wallsend Park and in 1912 remains of the east gate, found when Simpson's Hotel was built, were also transferred to the Park. Many Roman relics, coins and pottery have been found on the site and dateable evidence suggests occupation almost down to 400 A.D.

There appears to have been an extensive civilian settlement in the angle between the Wall and the fort stretching along the river bank. A bath-house, a temple and two or three streets have been recorded and there is evidence of a potter's kiln. Several early writers also noted remains of a possible Roman quay just below the fort.

The interior of the fort, as often happened, altered over the centuries and our reconstruction has tried to show Segedum in the 3rd century. It is based on information supplied to us by C. M. Daniels.

The Wall between Wallsend and Newcastle was 7 feet 6 inches wide on a foundation of 8 feet. Milecastle 1 (The Grange) is found 800 yards from the fort (Normally the distance is a Roman mile (1,620 yards).). Milecastle 2 (Walker) was a short distance east of the summit of Byker Hill, the Wall continuing over the highest part of the hill. Stukeley came here in 1725 and was so impressed with the view of the Wall from Byker Hill to Newcastle that he made a sketch of it which was published in his *Iter Boreale*, 1776, *View of the Tract of the Picts' Wall, Newcastleward, from Byker Mill Hill, 4 Sept.*, 1725. The Wall was then standing in good order. Ronald Embleton shows the same view in Roman times.

Milecastle 3 (Ouseburn) is shown on Stukeley's View. Milecastle 4 (Pilgrim Street) is conjectural.

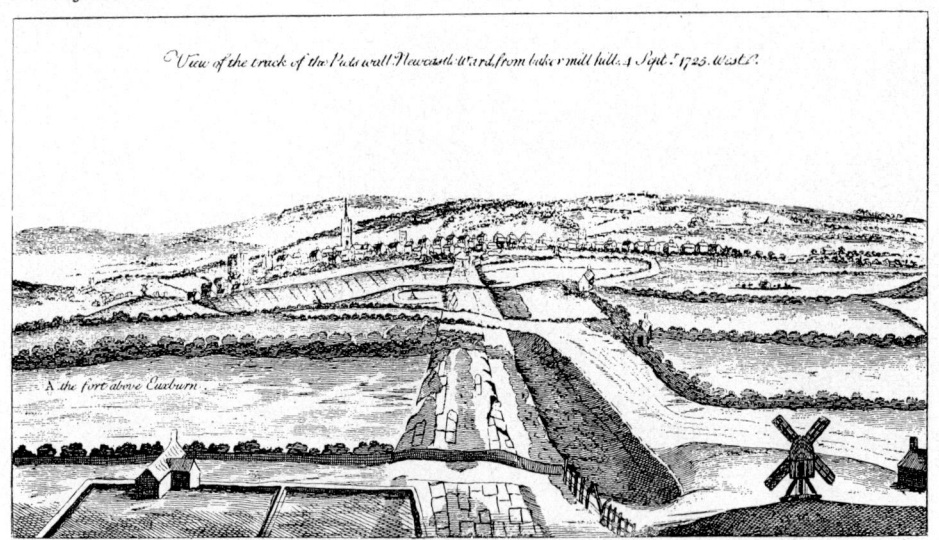

View from Byker Hill looking west 'A' marks the Ouseburn milecastle

South Shields Harbour

Roman skillet (*patera*) cast in bronze. Early 3rd century. Probably made in Gaul. Found in the wreck of a ship on the north sands at South Shields. *Paterae* were used for many purposes in Roman cookery, such as boiling stews and decocting wine, and sometimes had strainers. Each Roman soldier carried one.

Stone Mason's Workshop

Grinding corn on a mill

NEWCASTLE UPON TYNE (PONS AELIUS)

Newcastle was originally the beginning of the Wall. This is assumed because the stretch between Newcastle and Wallsend is the Narrow Wall and the stretch to the west is Broad Wall. The milecastles to the west are spaced exactly from the bridge. Probably the Romans found there was too much penetration by marauders down the denes between Newcastle and Wallsend so the Wall had to be extended.

We know the exact site of the bridge but the fort is not so certain. During their 400 years of occupation of the North the Romans built three bridges over the Tyne, one on practically the same site as the present Swing Bridge, the second at Corbridge and the third at Chesters. In the case of Newcastle the remains of only two piers have been found. However, two fine altars dedicated respectively to Neptune and Oceanus have been dredged from the river. They came from a shrine on the bridge, built by the Sixth Legion, to protect the structure from floods and tides.

The Newcastle Bridge was built by the Emporer Titus Aelius Hadrianus about 120 A.D. and was called Pons Aelius, and the camp guarding it received the same name. Few Roman frontier posts bear Imperial names. The length of the bridge to the banks of the river has been calculated at 735 feet. The piers were used later by the medieval bridge. Third pier from the south was found in 1872 when the Swing Bridge was being built.

The pier had a cutwater both up and down stream. Its width was 16 feet and the parallel sides were 20 feet long. The oak timbers, black with age, were found. They had been shod with iron and driven into the bed of the river. Heavy timber was laid across them to provide a foundation for the stone pier. There appear to have been ten piers and two abutments.

For long the site of the Roman fort has been a subject of controversy, however, recent excavations by Miss Barbara Harbottle show that the Castle Keep is on the site of the fort.

In the early 4th century the garrison was the First Cohort of Cornovii. This was the only British fort garrison on the wall. The Cornovii came fron the Cheshire, Staffordshire and Shropshire districts. A tablet recording work done by the 1st Cohort of Thracians has been found at Newcastle (south side of Hanover Square) but probably records only their work on the Vallum.

From Newcastle a road led south to Chester-le-street with an eastward branch to South Shields. It has also been suggested that a road ran north, joining the Devil's Causeway near its crossing of the Coquet.

The reconstruction by Ronald Embleton shows the chapel on the bridge at Pons Aelius. We have also reproduced H. B. Richardson's drawing made *c.* 1840. It is purely imaginary but very accurate bearing in mind that it was one of the earliest attempts to show Hadrian's Wall as it was originally.

A merchant's wife at South Shields

A jet worker at South Shields

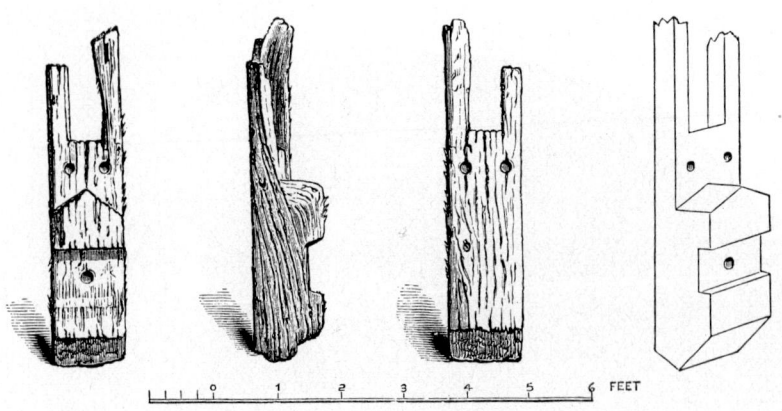

Roman timbers from the bridge at Newcastle

Roman altars which stood on bridge at Newcastle

The altar to Neptune reads: NEPTUNE LE(G10) VI VI(CTRIX) P(1A) F(IDELIS). *To Neptune, the 6th Legion, Victorious, Pious and Faithful.*

The altar to Ocean reads: OCIANO LEG(10) VI VI(CTRIX) P(1A) F(IDELIS). *To Ocean, the 6th Legion, Victorious, Pious and Faithful.*

Punishments in the Roman army were very severe. The soldier here being stoned to death outside the walls of Pons Aelius was probably guilty of cowardice.

Inscribed slab from the Tyne Bridge by Julius Verus c. 158 A.D.

BENWELL FORT (CONDERCUM)

The third fort on the Wall was Condercum standing near the top of Benwell Hill, with an extensive view in all directions. The distance from Newcastle is just over two miles and to Rudchester 6¾ miles. The reason why Benwell was built only two miles miles from Newcastle was probably because Newcastle was a very small fort only intended to defend the bridge and the first opportunity to erect a large fort was taken at Benwell. Today the northern part of the fort is covered by a reservoir and cut by the Newcastle-Carlisle road. About two thirds of the fort lies to the sout h of the road.

In the second century the first milliary cohort of the Vangiones was stationed here. In the *Notitia* the garrison is described as *Praefectus Alae primae Asturum Conderco*. The Astureans came from northern Spain. The term *ala* means a body of cavalry (in strength just over 500 men). Cavalry were chosen for Benwell because the flat open country here was suitable for their use. The Astureans were the garrison from A.D. 205 to 367. A dedication of about 240 has been preserved.

The fort measurements seem to have been about 570 feet from north to south and 400 feet east to west with an area of just over five acres. The fort was built in Hadrianic times and extensively rebuilt towards the end of the second century. It continued in occupation until late in the fourth century. It is a typical oblong fort with rounded angles.

The original building of the fort was carried out by the second legion as can be seen in a fine dedication, now in the British Museum. The stone bears the symbols of a Capricorn and a Pegasus confronting a *vexillum* (Standard).

Size, 1 foot 3 inches by 10 inches.

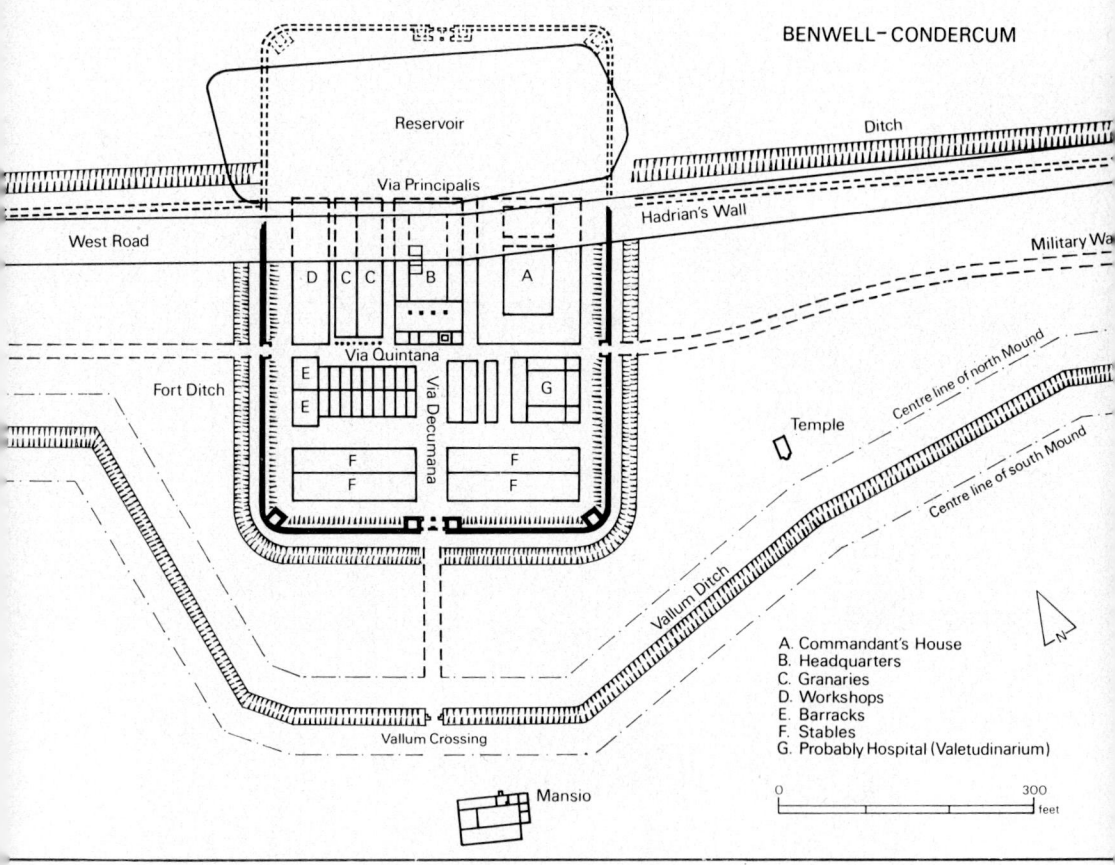

The most important remain to be seen at Benwell today is the Vallum crossing. The VALLUM can be traced right round Benwell fort. Only at Birdoswald can a similar diverted vallun be completely traced. The *vallum* at Benwell is however unique because the vallum crossing has been preserved and can be seen today. It is a causeway of un-dug earth the fort either existed or was planned before the vallum was built) with gaps through both mounds. The straight sides of the causeway were reverted in well dressed stone with a drain on each side of the southern section . In the centre of the crossing resting on the east and west revetments are the massive foundations of a gateway. The passage is 12 feet wide and was closed by two doors opening to the north. The massive foundations seen today would have been built up and joined by some form of arch making an imposing entrance. The vallum crossing here was used for a long time as successive periods of road are visible on the north looking like a series of steps.

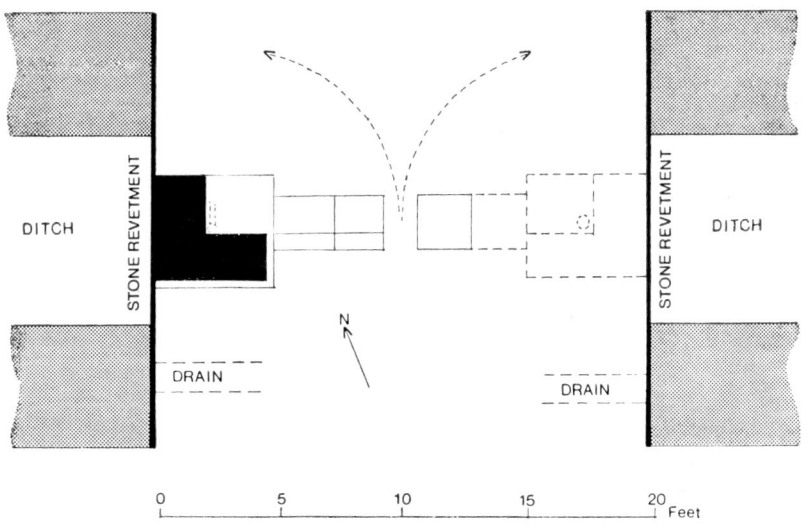

GATEWAY OF VALLUM CROSSING AT BENWELL

TEMPLE OF ANTENOCITICUS AT BENWELL

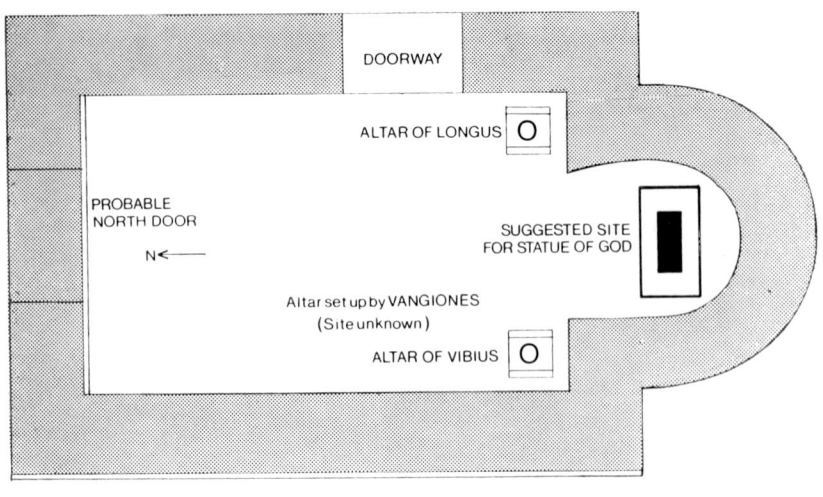

Temple of Antenociticus

Many gods were worshipped on the Roman Wall. Besides the official gods such as the soldiers' deities Mars and Hercules there were numerous native gods and foreign ones brought in by the auxiliary troops. Because of the variety there were no large temples but a multitude of smaller ones. The god at Benwell was Antenociticus who had his own temple, the remains of which can still be seen. There appears to have been a large civilian settlement at Benwell. The bath house was 300 yards south west of the fort, the *mansio* 300 yards to the south and the temple of Antenociticus 200 yards to the east. The Military Way was lined with buildings north and south of the vallum.

The temple of Antenociticus was discovered in 1862 in the grounds of Condercum House, south east of the fort within the line of the Vallum. It now lies in Broomridge Avenue open to view. The internal measurements are 18 by 10 feet plus the apse. The entrance is on the east but in its early form was probably on the north as shown in the plan. Two altars were found face down but *in situ*. Another altar in fragments was found but its original site in unknown. A full-size head with fragments of arm and leg was also found, almost certainly the statue of the god. It probably stood in the nave. Evidence from the excavation of the temple suggest it was deliberately destroyed late in the 2nd century and never rebuilt.

The interior view of the temple shows the two main altars (of Longus and Vibius) with the statue of the god in the apse. Only the head of the god has survived "ovoid in shape, with wild hair and Celtic neck torque." The floor was covered with fine sand. Whether Antenociticus was a local god or imported by the Vangiones we do not know. He has only been found at Benwell.

"To the god Anenociticus, Tineius Longus, who was given senatorial rank and appointed quaester designate while he.was cavalry prefect, by decree of our best and greatest emperors under the consul Ulpius Marcellus."

HOSPITAL (VALETUDINARIUM)

Few hospitals have been found in the auxiliary forts on the Wall but many had them, especially *ala* forts and *milliary* cohort forts. Probably a hospital provided medical treatment for a group of forts. There was almost certainly a hospital at Wallsend as well as the better known one at Benwell.

Doctors were of centurion rank and some have been recorded on tombstones. A doctor at Binchester, M. Aurelius Abrocomas, was doctor to a group of cavalry of Vettonians, and dedicated an altar to Aesculapius and Salus. Under the doctors were bandagers (*capsarii*) and orderlies (*medici*) who cared for the wounded on the battlefield and in hospitals. The doctors were fairly skilled since thet had plenyy of practise and a variety of medical instruments have been found on the Wall. Surgeons were held in more esteem than physicians, many of whom were quacks.

There is some evidence that medical herbs were grown on some sites for use by the garrison.

The hospital at Benwell stood behind the Commandant's house on the south side of the *via quintana* and measured 74 by 81 feet. This quiet and secluded position was usually chosen for a hospital because the rest of the fort was very noisy. Although never completely excavated due to the presence of modern buildings, it was revealed as a courtyard building with the wings divided into small rooms.

Anaesthetics were limited and consisted largely of preparations made from poppy, henbane and mandrake. The Roman medical writer Celsus says that a good surgeon should learn to ignore the cries of his patient.

A Roman Bakery

There was a large civilian settlement at Benwell since the site was pleasant and fertile. The Roman road behind the Wall was lined with buildings. There were several temples, an inn for travellers, and a bathhouse whose plan has been preserved.

Benwell however is of great social interest because here coal was first mined and used for industrial purposes. In the fort workshops coal has been found which probably came from open-cast workings nearby.

From Benwell the Roman Wall follows the line of the main Carlisle road. The area is now built up but in Roman times was open country. Between the *vicus* of Condercum and the fort of Vindolanda (Rudchester) there were no civilian settlements for almost 7 miles. An observant traveller would however have noticed almost midway between two milecastles (now designated 7 and 8) a fine culvert under the Wall which carried the stream now called the Denton Burn. In 1867 Bruce recorded this culvert, which was the only one left on the entire Wall, and probably identical with many others built where streams crossed the mural barrier.

Culvert at Denton Burn

The rounded arch is 18th century. The Roman work is in large stones.

A Potter at Work

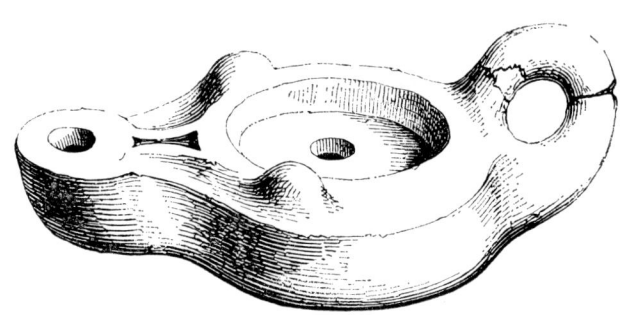

Roman Oil Lamp

ass produced pottery was brought to the *vici*
e Wall from the south but some pottery was
uced locally, especially at Corbridge where
is evidence that it was made on a large scale.
tter's kiln was traced in the *vicus* at Wallsend.

Below: Monumental slab from the Granary

Making Charcoal

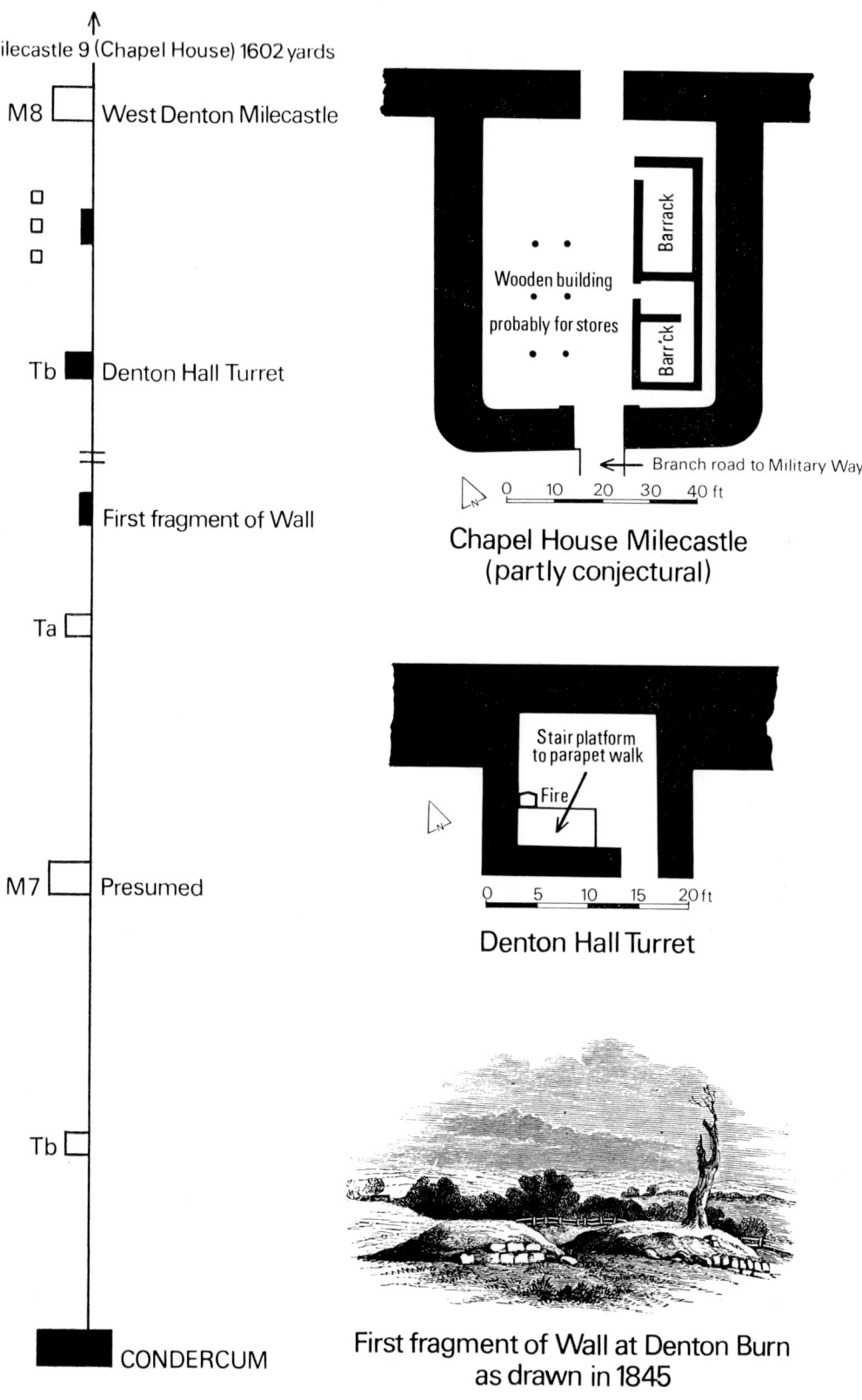

HADRIAN'S WALL IN THE DAYS OF THE ROMANS

Publication date 1983

This booklet is the third in our series describing the Roman Wall in the time of the Romans. The other two describe Housesteads (today the best preserved of the Wall forts), and Chester and Carrawburgh. Our fourth book will describe the Stanegate which ran from Corbridge to Carlisle. It will deal especially with the town of Corbridge, the fort at Vindolanda (with its famous *vicus*) and Carvoran.

The booklets are part of a major work we are preparing which will describe the entire Wall in the days when the frontier defences flourished.

The Roman Wall was occupied for almost three hundred years and during that time it was altered, destroyed, and rebuilt on more than one occasion. To show the whole Wall at a particular time in its history would be an impossible task, so the present booklet and the final *magnum opus* describe facets of life on the Wall at various periods.

The complete work will contain approximately 80 full page colour plates and 250 illustrations in black and white. Every aspect of Roman life will be described with reconstructions not only of buildings but of the everyday life of the soldiers and civilians. Never before has such a grand attempt been made to show in vivid colourful detail the life of Roman Britain.

Although sections of our work will only apply to Hadrian's Wall the book will show what life was like on most Roman frontiers. The civilian section of the book will describe the social conditions, customs, trade and commerce which prevailed in many areas of Roman settlement on our island.

The final work will therefore be a fairly comprehensive social and military survey of most of Roman Britain. We hope to publish the book in 1983.